For chapters that are more narrative in structure (tell a story, follow a person, etc) you might want to use this narrative chapter bookmark.

Cut it out and use it to mark your place in the book and use as needed on the chapters that don't have a verse that stands out to you.

You can also find a free printable of this (so you can print it on cardstock) on my website under the Subscriber Bonuses tab after you subscribe. www.stonesoupforfive.com.

Bible Reading and Meditation Journal

narrative chapter options

Summarize
(keep this box the same)

Who?
(replaces: Verses that stood out)
Who wrote this?
Who is in this chapter?
What do the main people do?
What do they say?

What?
(replaces: Why did I pick this verse)
What is going on in the chapter?
Is there anything going wrong?

When? Where?
(replaces: Definitions of words)
When does this happen?
What came before?
Is there a time of day?
A special date?
Where did it happen?

Why?
(replaces: Rewrite the verse in your own words)
This is the most important question.
Why is this chapter in the Bible?
Why did these events happen?
Why do the characters act/react this way?
Keep asking why.

Wherefore?
(replaces: Does this verse reveal anything...)
What does this chapter have to teach me?
What does it show me?
What does it teach about God/Jesus/Holy Spirit?

How can I apply insights...
(keep this box the same)

Notes, quotes, etc...
(keep this box the same)

Welcome!

This Biblical Meditation Series is designed to help you meditate through the entire Bible in about three years. The series will help you read through each chapter of the Bible at a pace that allows you to meditate, apply, pray, and enjoy your time in the Word. And, at the end of the series, you will have created your own personal commentary of your time spent in the Bible.

The series starts here, with Volume One. In this volume we will start by reading through the history of Jesus as told in the book of Matthew. After that introduction, we will move into the Old Testament starting in Genesis and moving through part of Exodus. Each volume will take you through a quarter of a year but can be started at any time.

Each day you work in this book, you will read the chapter (or short chapters) written at the top of the page, then you'll fill in each of the boxes on the two-page spread for that day. There is a page for each Monday through Saturday for you to work in, and on Sunday there are two pages for reflection on the previous week's work.

My hope and prayer is that as you work through these pages you'll have time to slow down and think deeply about the truth in the Bible and how it applies to your life and your growth as His child.

For more tools, inspiration, and ideas on how to use this guide, visit my website at: www.stonesoupforfive.com.

You can also find me on Facebook at www.facebook.com/StoneSoupForFive and you can join a community of people growing together at our private (free) Facebook group here: https://www.facebook.com/groups/journalanddoodle/

Matthew 1

Date:

Summarize the main idea(s) in this chapter:

Verse(s) that stood out:

Why did I pick this verse?

Definitions of words and/or cross references from my verse:

Rewrite the verse in your own words or personalize it.

Does this verse reveal anything about God/Jesus/Holy Spirit? Are there examples to follow or avoid?

How can I apply insights from this verse today? This week?

Notes, quotes, doodles, checklists, prayers, etc.

Matthew 2

Date:

Summarize the main idea(s) in this chapter:

Verse(s) that stood out:

Why did I pick this verse?

Definitions of words and/or cross references from my verse:

Rewrite the verse in your own words or personalize it.

Does this verse reveal anything about God/Jesus/Holy Spirit? Are there examples to follow or avoid?

How can I apply insights from this verse today? This week?

Notes, quotes, doodles, checklists, prayers, etc.

 # Matthew 3

Date:

Summarize the main idea(s) in this chapter:

Verse(s) that stood out:

Why did I pick this verse?

Definitions of words and/or cross references from my verse:

Rewrite the verse in your own words or personalize it.

Does this verse reveal anything about God/Jesus/Holy Spirit? Are there examples to follow or avoid?

How can I apply insights from this verse today? This week?

Notes, quotes, doodles, checklists, prayers, etc.

Date:

Summarize the main idea(s) in this chapter:

Verse(s) that stood out:

Why did I pick this verse?

Definitions of words and/or cross references from my verse:

Rewrite the verse in your own words or personalize it.

Does this verse reveal anything about God/Jesus/Holy Spirit? Are there examples to follow or avoid?

How can I apply insights from this verse today? This week?

Notes, quotes, doodles, checklists, prayers, etc.

Summarize the main idea(s) in this chapter:

Verse(s) that stood out:

Why did I pick this verse?

Definitions of words and/or cross references from my verse:

Rewrite the verse in your own words or personalize it.

Does this verse reveal anything about God/Jesus/Holy Spirit? Are there examples to follow or avoid?

How can I apply insights from this verse today? This week?

Notes, quotes, doodles, checklists, prayers, etc.

Matthew 6

Date:

Summarize the main idea(s) in this chapter:

Verse(s) that stood out:

Why did I pick this verse?

Definitions of words and/or cross references from my verse:

Rewrite the verse in your own words or personalize it.

Does this verse reveal anything about God/Jesus/Holy Spirit? Are there examples to follow or avoid?

How can I apply insights from this verse today? This week?

Notes, quotes, doodles, checklists, prayers, etc.

Review and reflect

Review each of the last six days work. Write or list the main takeaway you got from each chapter. (Look closely at the sections "What does this reveal about God?" and "How can I apply this?")

Are there any themes showing up in this week's work?

Are there any areas God is wanting to grow my faith or trust?
Are there any insights from this week's work on how to do this?

Are there any sins God is spotlighting in my life?
Are there any insights from this week's work on how to kill these sins?

Re-read one or two of the most impactful verses from this week and turn them into a prayer. (There is room on the next pages to write it down if you want.)

How can I thank or praise God as a result of what I've learned this week?

How can I apply what I've learned this week to my life today and next week?

Where do I need His strength for today? Tomorrow? Next week?

Is there a verse from this week that I should commit to memory? Write it on the next page or on a 3x5 card to take with you to memorize.

Are there any sins I need to confess to God in prayer?

Is there anyone I need to forgive? Is there anyone I need to ask forgiveness of?

Are there any seeds of bitterness starting to take root in my heart?

Are there any fears or worries I need to lay at His feet?

prayers, doodles, etc

 **Matthew 7**

Date:

Summarize the main idea(s) in this chapter:

Verse(s) that stood out:

Why did I pick this verse?

Definitions of words and/or cross references from my verse:

Rewrite the verse in your own words or personalize it.

Does this verse reveal anything about God/Jesus/Holy Spirit? Are there examples to follow or avoid?

How can I apply insights from this verse today? This week?

Notes, quotes, doodles, checklists, prayers, etc.

Matthew 8

Date:

Summarize the main idea(s) in this chapter:

Verse(s) that stood out:

Why did I pick this verse?

Definitions of words and/or cross references from my verse:

Rewrite the verse in your own words or personalize it.

Does this verse reveal anything about God/Jesus/Holy Spirit? Are there examples to follow or avoid?

How can I apply insights from this verse today? This week?

Notes, quotes, doodles, checklists, prayers, etc.

Matthew 9

Date:

Summarize the main idea(s) in this chapter:

Verse(s) that stood out:

Why did I pick this verse?

Definitions of words and/or cross references from my verse:

Rewrite the verse in your own words or personalize it.

Does this verse reveal anything about God/Jesus/Holy Spirit? Are there examples to follow or avoid?

How can I apply insights from this verse today? This week?

Notes, quotes, doodles, checklists, prayers, etc.

Matthew 10

Date:

Summarize the main idea(s) in this chapter:

Verse(s) that stood out:

Why did I pick this verse?

Definitions of words and/or cross references from my verse:

Rewrite the verse in your own words or personalize it.

Does this verse reveal anything about God/Jesus/Holy Spirit? Are there examples to follow or avoid?

How can I apply insights from this verse today? This week?

Notes, quotes, doodles, checklists, prayers, etc.

 Matthew 11

Date:

Summarize the main idea(s) in this chapter:

Verse(s) that stood out:

Why did I pick this verse?

Definitions of words and/or cross references from my verse:

Rewrite the verse in your own words or personalize it.

Does this verse reveal anything about God/Jesus/Holy Spirit? Are there examples to follow or avoid?

How can I apply insights from this verse today? This week?

Notes, quotes, doodles, checklists, prayers, etc.

# Matthew 12

Date:

Summarize the main idea(s) in this chapter:

Verse(s) that stood out:

Why did I pick this verse?

Definitions of words and/or cross references from my verse:

Rewrite the verse in your own words or personalize it.

Does this verse reveal anything about God/Jesus/Holy Spirit? Are there examples to follow or avoid?

How can I apply insights from this verse today? This week?

Notes, quotes, doodles, checklists, prayers, etc.

Review and reflect

Date:

Review each of the last six days work. Write or list the main takeaway you got from each chapter. (Look closely at the sections "What does this reveal about God?" and "How can I apply this?")

Are there any themes showing up in this week's work?

Are there any areas God is wanting to grow my faith or trust?
Are there any insights from this week's work on how to do this?

Are there any sins God is spotlighting in my life?
Are there any insights from this week's work on how to kill these sins?

Re-read one or two of the most impactful verses from this week and turn them into a prayer. (There is room on the next pages to write it down if you want.)

How can I thank or praise God as a result of what I've learned this week?

How can I apply what I've learned this week to my life today and next week?

Where do I need His strength for today? Tomorrow? Next week?

Is there a verse from this week that I should commit to memory? Write it on the next page or on a 3x5 card to take with you to memorize.

Are there any sins I need to confess to God in prayer?

Is there anyone I need to forgive? Is there anyone I need to ask forgiveness of?

Are there any seeds of bitterness starting to take root in my heart?

Are there any fears or worries I need to lay at His feet?

notes, verses to memorize

prayers, doodles, etc

Date:

Summarize the main idea(s) in this chapter:

Verse(s) that stood out:

Why did I pick this verse?

Definitions of words and/or cross references from my verse:

Rewrite the verse in your own words or personalize it.

Does this verse reveal anything about God/Jesus/Holy Spirit? Are there examples to follow or avoid?

How can I apply insights from this verse today? This week?

Notes, quotes, doodles, checklists, prayers, etc.

Matthew 14

Date:

Summarize the main idea(s) in this chapter:

Verse(s) that stood out:

Why did I pick this verse?

Definitions of words and/or cross references from my verse:

Rewrite the verse in your own words or personalize it.

Does this verse reveal anything about God/Jesus/Holy Spirit? Are there examples to follow or avoid?

How can I apply insights from this verse today? This week?

Notes, quotes, doodles, checklists, prayers, etc.

Matthew 15

Date:

Summarize the main idea(s) in this chapter:

Verse(s) that stood out:

Why did I pick this verse?

Definitions of words and/or cross references from my verse:

Rewrite the verse in your own words or personalize it.

Does this verse reveal anything about God/Jesus/Holy Spirit? Are there examples to follow or avoid?

How can I apply insights from this verse today? This week?

Notes, quotes, doodles, checklists, prayers, etc.

Date:

Summarize the main idea(s) in this chapter:

Verse(s) that stood out:

Why did I pick this verse?

Definitions of words and/or cross references from my verse:

Rewrite the verse in your own words or personalize it.

Does this verse reveal anything about God/Jesus/Holy Spirit? Are there examples to follow or avoid?

How can I apply insights from this verse today? This week?

Notes, quotes, doodles, checklists, prayers, etc.

Matthew 17

Date:

Summarize the main idea(s) in this chapter:

Verse(s) that stood out:

Why did I pick this verse?

Definitions of words and/or cross references from my verse:

Rewrite the verse in your own words or personalize it.

Does this verse reveal anything about God/Jesus/Holy Spirit? Are there examples to follow or avoid?

How can I apply insights from this verse today? This week?

Notes, quotes, doodles, checklists, prayers, etc.

 *Matthew 18*

Summarize the main idea(s) in this chapter:

Verse(s) that stood out:

Why did I pick this verse?

Definitions of words and/or cross references from my verse:

Rewrite the verse in your own words or personalize it.

Does this verse reveal anything about God/Jesus/Holy Spirit? Are there examples to follow or avoid?

How can I apply insights from this verse today? This week?

Notes, quotes, doodles, checklists, prayers, etc.

Review and reflect

Date:

Review each of the last six days work. Write or list the main takeaway you got from each chapter. (Look closely at the sections "What does this reveal about God?" and "How can I apply this?")

Are there any themes showing up in this week's work?

Are there any areas God is wanting to grow my faith or trust?
Are there any insights from this week's work on how to do this?

Are there any sins God is spotlighting in my life?
Are there any insights from this week's work on how to kill these sins?

Re-read one or two of the most impactful verses from this week and turn them into a prayer. (There is room on the next pages to write it down if you want.)

How can I thank or praise God as a result of what I've learned this week?

How can I apply what I've learned this week to my life today and next week?

Where do I need His strength for today? Tomorrow? Next week?

Is there a verse from this week that I should commit to memory? Write it on the next page or on a 3x5 card to take with you to memorize.

Are there any sins I need to confess to God in prayer?

Is there anyone I need to forgive? Is there anyone I need to ask forgiveness of?

Are there any seeds of bitterness starting to take root in my heart?

Are there any fears or worries I need to lay at His feet?

notes, verses to memorize

prayers, doodles, etc

 **Matthew 19**

Date:

Summarize the main idea(s) in this chapter:

Verse(s) that stood out:

Why did I pick this verse?

Definitions of words and/or cross references from my verse:

Rewrite the verse in your own words or personalize it.

Does this verse reveal anything about God/Jesus/Holy Spirit? Are there examples to follow or avoid?

How can I apply insights from this verse today? This week?

Notes, quotes, doodles, checklists, prayers, etc.

Date:

Summarize the main idea(s) in this chapter:

Verse(s) that stood out:

Why did I pick this verse?

Definitions of words and/or cross references from my verse:

Rewrite the verse in your own words or personalize it.

Does this verse reveal anything about God/Jesus/Holy Spirit? Are there examples to follow or avoid?

How can I apply insights from this verse today? This week?

Notes, quotes, doodles, checklists, prayers, etc.

 Matthew 21

Date:

Summarize the main idea(s) in this chapter:

Verse(s) that stood out:

Why did I pick this verse?

Definitions of words and/or cross references from my verse:

Rewrite the verse in your own words or personalize it.

Does this verse reveal anything about God/Jesus/Holy Spirit? Are there examples to follow or avoid?

How can I apply insights from this verse today? This week?

Notes, quotes, doodles, checklists, prayers, etc.

 **Matthew 22**

Date:

Summarize the main idea(s) in this chapter:

Verse(s) that stood out:

Why did I pick this verse?

Definitions of words and/or cross references from my verse:

Rewrite the verse in your own words or personalize it.

Does this verse reveal anything about God/Jesus/Holy Spirit? Are there examples to follow or avoid?

How can I apply insights from this verse today? This week?

Notes, quotes, doodles, checklists, prayers, etc.

Matthew 23

Date:

Summarize the main idea(s) in this chapter:

Verse(s) that stood out:

Why did I pick this verse?

Definitions of words and/or cross references from my verse:

Rewrite the verse in your own words or personalize it.

Does this verse reveal anything about God/Jesus/Holy Spirit? Are there examples to follow or avoid?

How can I apply insights from this verse today? This week?

Notes, quotes, doodles, checklists, prayers, etc.

Date:

Summarize the main idea(s) in this chapter:

Verse(s) that stood out:

Why did I pick this verse?

Definitions of words and/or cross references from my verse:

Rewrite the verse in your own words or personalize it.

Does this verse reveal anything about God/Jesus/Holy Spirit? Are there examples to follow or avoid?

How can I apply insights from this verse today? This week?

Notes, quotes, doodles, checklists, prayers, etc.

Review and reflect

Review each of the last six days work. Write or list the main takeaway you got from each chapter. (Look closely at the sections "What does this reveal about God?" and "How can I apply this?")

Are there any themes showing up in this week's work?

Are there any areas God is wanting to grow my faith or trust?
Are there any insights from this week's work on how to do this?

Are there any sins God is spotlighting in my life?
Are there any insights from this week's work on how to kill these sins?

Re-read one or two of the most impactful verses from this week and turn them into a prayer. (There is room on the next pages to write it down if you want.)

How can I thank or praise God as a result of what I've learned this week?

_____

_____

_____

_____

How can I apply what I've learned this week to my life today and next week?

_____

_____

_____

_____

_____

Where do I need His strength for today? Tomorrow? Next week?

_____

_____

_____

_____

_____

_____

Is there a verse from this week that I should commit to memory? Write it on the next page or on a 3x5 card to take with you to memorize.

Are there any sins I need to confess to God in prayer?

Is there anyone I need to forgive? Is there anyone I need to ask forgiveness of?

Are there any seeds of bitterness starting to take root in my heart?

Are there any fears or worries I need to lay at His feet?

prayers, doodles, etc

 **Matthew 25**

Date:

Summarize the main idea(s) in this chapter:

Verse(s) that stood out:

Why did I pick this verse?

Definitions of words and/or cross references from my verse:

Rewrite the verse in your own words or personalize it.

Does this verse reveal anything about God/Jesus/Holy Spirit? Are there examples to follow or avoid?

How can I apply insights from this verse today? This week?

Notes, quotes, doodles, checklists, prayers, etc.

Date:

Summarize the main idea(s) in this chapter:

Verse(s) that stood out:

Why did I pick this verse?

Definitions of words and/or cross references from my verse:

Rewrite the verse in your own words or personalize it.

Does this verse reveal anything about God/Jesus/Holy Spirit? Are there examples to follow or avoid?

How can I apply insights from this verse today? This week?

Notes, quotes, doodles, checklists, prayers, etc.

Date:

Summarize the main idea(s) in this chapter:

Verse(s) that stood out:

Why did I pick this verse?

Definitions of words and/or cross references from my verse:

Rewrite the verse in your own words or personalize it.

Does this verse reveal anything about God/Jesus/Holy Spirit? Are there examples to follow or avoid?

How can I apply insights from this verse today? This week?

Notes, quotes, doodles, checklists, prayers, etc.

Matthew 28

Date:

Summarize the main idea(s) in this chapter:

Verse(s) that stood out:

Why did I pick this verse?

Definitions of words and/or cross references from my verse:

Rewrite the verse in your own words or personalize it.

Does this verse reveal anything about God/Jesus/Holy Spirit? Are there examples to follow or avoid?

How can I apply insights from this verse today? This week?

Notes, quotes, doodles, checklists, prayers, etc.

Genesis 1

Date:

Summarize the main idea(s) in this chapter:

Verse(s) that stood out:

Why did I pick this verse?

Definitions of words and/or cross references from my verse:

Rewrite the verse in your own words or personalize it.

Does this verse reveal anything about God/Jesus/Holy Spirit? Are there examples to follow or avoid?

How can I apply insights from this verse today? This week?

Notes, quotes, doodles, checklists, prayers, etc.

Genesis 2-3

Summarize the main idea(s) in this chapter:

Verse(s) that stood out:

Why did I pick this verse?

Definitions of words and/or cross references from my verse:

Rewrite the verse in your own words or personalize it.

Does this verse reveal anything about God/Jesus/Holy Spirit? Are there examples to follow or avoid?

How can I apply insights from this verse today? This week?

Notes, quotes, doodles, checklists, prayers, etc.

Review and reflect

Date:

Review each of the last six days work. Write or list the main takeaway you got from each chapter. (Look closely at the sections "What does this reveal about God?" and "How can I apply this?")

Are there any themes showing up in this week's work?

Are there any areas God is wanting to grow my faith or trust?
Are there any insights from this week's work on how to do this?

Are there any sins God is spotlighting in my life?
Are there any insights from this week's work on how to kill these sins?

Re-read one or two of the most impactful verses from this week and turn them into a prayer. (There is room on the next pages to write it down if you want.)

How can I thank or praise God as a result of what I've learned this week?

How can I apply what I've learned this week to my life today and next week?

Where do I need His strength for today? Tomorrow? Next week?

Is there a verse from this week that I should commit to memory? Write it on the next page or on a 3x5 card to take with you to memorize.

Are there any sins I need to confess to God in prayer?

Is there anyone I need to forgive? Is there anyone I need to ask forgiveness of?

Are there any seeds of bitterness starting to take root in my heart?

Are there any fears or worries I need to lay at His feet?

notes, verses to memorize

prayers, doodles, etc

Genesis 4

Date:

Summarize the main idea(s) in this chapter:

Verse(s) that stood out:

Why did I pick this verse?

Definitions of words and/or cross references from my verse:

Rewrite the verse in your own words or personalize it.

Does this verse reveal anything about God/Jesus/Holy Spirit? Are there examples to follow or avoid?

How can I apply insights from this verse today? This week?

Notes, quotes, doodles, checklists, prayers, etc.

Genesis 5

Date:

Summarize the main idea(s) in this chapter:

Verse(s) that stood out:

Why did I pick this verse?

Definitions of words and/or cross references from my verse:

Rewrite the verse in your own words or personalize it.

Does this verse reveal anything about God/Jesus/Holy Spirit? Are there examples to follow or avoid?

How can I apply insights from this verse today? This week?

Notes, quotes, doodles, checklists, prayers, etc.

Genesis 6-7

Summarize the main idea(s) in this chapter:

Verse(s) that stood out:

Why did I pick this verse?

Definitions of words and/or cross references from my verse:

Rewrite the verse in your own words or personalize it.

Does this verse reveal anything about God/Jesus/Holy Spirit? Are there examples to follow or avoid?

How can I apply insights from this verse today? This week?

Notes, quotes, doodles, checklists, prayers, etc.

Genesis 8-9

Summarize the main idea(s) in this chapter:

Verse(s) that stood out:

Why did I pick this verse?

Definitions of words and/or cross references from my verse:

Rewrite the verse in your own words or personalize it.

Does this verse reveal anything about God/Jesus/Holy Spirit? Are there examples to follow or avoid?

How can I apply insights from this verse today? This week?

Notes, quotes, doodles, checklists, prayers, etc.

Genesis 10

Date:

Summarize the main idea(s) in this chapter:

Verse(s) that stood out:

Why did I pick this verse?

Definitions of words and/or cross references from my verse:

Rewrite the verse in your own words or personalize it.

Does this verse reveal anything about God/Jesus/Holy Spirit? Are there examples to follow or avoid?

How can I apply insights from this verse today? This week?

Notes, quotes, doodles, checklists, prayers, etc.

Genesis 11

Date:

Summarize the main idea(s) in this chapter:

Verse(s) that stood out:

Why did I pick this verse?

Definitions of words and/or cross references from my verse:

Rewrite the verse in your own words or personalize it.

Does this verse reveal anything about God/Jesus/Holy Spirit? Are there examples to follow or avoid?

How can I apply insights from this verse today? This week?

Notes, quotes, doodles, checklists, prayers, etc.

Review and reflect

Date:

Review each of the last six days work. Write or list the main takeaway you got from each chapter. (Look closely at the sections "What does this reveal about God?" and "How can I apply this?")

Are there any themes showing up in this week's work?

Are there any areas God is wanting to grow my faith or trust?
Are there any insights from this week's work on how to do this?

Are there any sins God is spotlighting in my life?
Are there any insights from this week's work on how to kill these sins?

Re-read one or two of the most impactful verses from this week and turn them into a prayer. (There is room on the next pages to write it down if you want.)

How can I thank or praise God as a result of what I've learned this week?

How can I apply what I've learned this week to my life today and next week?

Where do I need His strength for today? Tomorrow? Next week?

Is there a verse from this week that I should commit to memory? Write it on the next page or on a 3x5 card to take with you to memorize.

Are there any sins I need to confess to God in prayer?

Is there anyone I need to forgive? Is there anyone I need to ask forgiveness of?

Are there any seeds of bitterness starting to take root in my heart?

Are there any fears or worries I need to lay at His feet?

prayers, doodles, etc

Genesis 12-13

Date:

Summarize the main idea(s) in this chapter:

Verse(s) that stood out:

Why did I pick this verse?

Definitions of words and/or cross references from my verse:

Rewrite the verse in your own words or personalize it.

Does this verse reveal anything about God/Jesus/Holy Spirit? Are there examples to follow or avoid?

How can I apply insights from this verse today? This week?

Notes, quotes, doodles, checklists, prayers, etc.

Genesis 14-15

Date:

Summarize the main idea(s) in this chapter:

Verse(s) that stood out:

Why did I pick this verse?

Definitions of words and/or cross references from my verse:

Rewrite the verse in your own words or personalize it.

Does this verse reveal anything about God/Jesus/Holy Spirit? Are there examples to follow or avoid?

How can I apply insights from this verse today? This week?

Notes, quotes, doodles, checklists, prayers, etc.

Genesis 16-17

Date:

Summarize the main idea(s) in this chapter:

Verse(s) that stood out:

Why did I pick this verse?

Definitions of words and/or cross references from my verse:

Rewrite the verse in your own words or personalize it.

Does this verse reveal anything about God/Jesus/Holy Spirit? Are there examples to follow or avoid?

How can I apply insights from this verse today? This week?

Notes, quotes, doodles, checklists, prayers, etc.

Genesis 18

Summarize the main idea(s) in this chapter:

Verse(s) that stood out:

Why did I pick this verse?

Definitions of words and/or cross references from my verse:

Rewrite the verse in your own words or personalize it.

Does this verse reveal anything about God/Jesus/Holy Spirit? Are there examples to follow or avoid?

How can I apply insights from this verse today? This week?

Notes, quotes, doodles, checklists, prayers, etc.

Genesis 19

Date:

Summarize the main idea(s) in this chapter:

Verse(s) that stood out:

Why did I pick this verse?

Definitions of words and/or cross references from my verse:

Rewrite the verse in your own words or personalize it.

Does this verse reveal anything about God/Jesus/Holy Spirit? Are there examples to follow or avoid?

How can I apply insights from this verse today? This week?

Notes, quotes, doodles, checklists, prayers, etc.

Summarize the main idea(s) in this chapter:

Verse(s) that stood out:

Why did I pick this verse?

Definitions of words and/or cross references from my verse:

Rewrite the verse in your own words or personalize it.

Does this verse reveal anything about God/Jesus/Holy Spirit? Are there examples to follow or avoid?

How can I apply insights from this verse today? This week?

Notes, quotes, doodles, checklists, prayers, etc.

Review and reflect

Date:

Review each of the last six days work. Write or list the main takeaway you got from each chapter. (Look closely at the sections "What does this reveal about God?" and "How can I apply this?")

Are there any themes showing up in this week's work?

Are there any areas God is wanting to grow my faith or trust?
Are there any insights from this week's work on how to do this?

Are there any sins God is spotlighting in my life?
Are there any insights from this week's work on how to kill these sins?

Re-read one or two of the most impactful verses from this week and turn them into a prayer. (There is room on the next pages to write it down if you want.)

How can I thank or praise God as a result of what I've learned this week?

How can I apply what I've learned this week to my life today and next week?

Where do I need His strength for today? Tomorrow? Next week?

Is there a verse from this week that I should commit to memory? Write it on the next page or on a 3x5 card to take with you to memorize.

Are there any sins I need to confess to God in prayer?

Is there anyone I need to forgive? Is there anyone I need to ask forgiveness of?

Are there any seeds of bitterness starting to take root in my heart?

Are there any fears or worries I need to lay at His feet?

prayers, doodles, etc

Genesis 22-23

Date:

Summarize the main idea(s) in this chapter:

Verse(s) that stood out:

Why did I pick this verse?

Definitions of words and/or cross references from my verse:

Rewrite the verse in your own words or personalize it.

Does this verse reveal anything about God/Jesus/Holy Spirit? Are there examples to follow or avoid?

How can I apply insights from this verse today? This week?

Notes, quotes, doodles, checklists, prayers, etc.

Genesis 24

Date:

Summarize the main idea(s) in this chapter:

Verse(s) that stood out:

Why did I pick this verse?

Definitions of words and/or cross references from my verse:

Rewrite the verse in your own words or personalize it.

Does this verse reveal anything about God/Jesus/Holy Spirit? Are there examples to follow or avoid?

How can I apply insights from this verse today? This week?

Notes, quotes, doodles, checklists, prayers, etc.

Genesis 25

Summarize the main idea(s) in this chapter:

Verse(s) that stood out:

Why did I pick this verse?

Definitions of words and/or cross references from my verse:

Rewrite the verse in your own words or personalize it.

Does this verse reveal anything about God/Jesus/Holy Spirit? Are there examples to follow or avoid?

How can I apply insights from this verse today? This week?

Notes, quotes, doodles, checklists, prayers, etc.

Genesis 26

Summarize the main idea(s) in this chapter:

Verse(s) that stood out:

Why did I pick this verse?

Definitions of words and/or cross references from my verse:

Rewrite the verse in your own words or personalize it.

Does this verse reveal anything about God/Jesus/Holy Spirit? Are there examples to follow or avoid?

How can I apply insights from this verse today? This week?

Notes, quotes, doodles, checklists, prayers, etc.

Genesis 27

Date:

Summarize the main idea(s) in this chapter:

Verse(s) that stood out:

Why did I pick this verse?

Definitions of words and/or cross references from my verse:

Rewrite the verse in your own words or personalize it.

Does this verse reveal anything about God/Jesus/Holy Spirit? Are there examples to follow or avoid?

How can I apply insights from this verse today? This week?

Notes, quotes, doodles, checklists, prayers, etc.

Genesis 28

Summarize the main idea(s) in this chapter:

Verse(s) that stood out:

Why did I pick this verse?

Definitions of words and/or cross references from my verse:

Rewrite the verse in your own words or personalize it.

Does this verse reveal anything about God/Jesus/Holy Spirit? Are there examples to follow or avoid?

How can I apply insights from this verse today? This week?

Notes, quotes, doodles, checklists, prayers, etc.

Review and reflect

Date:

Review each of the last six days work. Write or list the main takeaway you got from each chapter. (Look closely at the sections "What does this reveal about God?" and "How can I apply this?")

Are there any themes showing up in this week's work?

Are there any areas God is wanting to grow my faith or trust?
Are there any insights from this week's work on how to do this?

Are there any sins God is spotlighting in my life?
Are there any insights from this week's work on how to kill these sins?

Re-read one or two of the most impactful verses from this week and turn them into a prayer. (There is room on the next pages to write it down if you want.)

How can I thank or praise God as a result of what I've learned this week?

How can I apply what I've learned this week to my life today and next week?

Where do I need His strength for today? Tomorrow? Next week?

Is there a verse from this week that I should commit to memory? Write it on the next page or on a 3x5 card to take with you to memorize.

Are there any sins I need to confess to God in prayer?

Is there anyone I need to forgive? Is there anyone I need to ask forgiveness of?

Are there any seeds of bitterness starting to take root in my heart?

Are there any fears or worries I need to lay at His feet?

prayers, doodles, etc

Genesis 29

Date:

Summarize the main idea(s) in this chapter:

Verse(s) that stood out:

Why did I pick this verse?

Definitions of words and/or cross references from my verse:

Rewrite the verse in your own words or personalize it.

Does this verse reveal anything about God/Jesus/Holy Spirit? Are there examples to follow or avoid?

How can I apply insights from this verse today? This week?

Notes, quotes, doodles, checklists, prayers, etc.

Genesis 30

Date:

Summarize the main idea(s) in this chapter:

Verse(s) that stood out:

Why did I pick this verse?

Definitions of words and/or cross references from my verse:

Rewrite the verse in your own words or personalize it.

Does this verse reveal anything about God/Jesus/Holy Spirit? Are there examples to follow or avoid?

How can I apply insights from this verse today? This week?

Notes, quotes, doodles, checklists, prayers, etc.

Genesis 31

Date:

Summarize the main idea(s) in this chapter:

Verse(s) that stood out:

Why did I pick this verse?

Definitions of words and/or cross references from my verse:

Rewrite the verse in your own words or personalize it.

Does this verse reveal anything about God/Jesus/Holy Spirit? Are there examples to follow or avoid?

How can I apply insights from this verse today? This week?

Notes, quotes, doodles, checklists, prayers, etc.

Genesis 32-33

Date:

Summarize the main idea(s) in this chapter:

Verse(s) that stood out:

Why did I pick this verse?

Definitions of words and/or cross references from my verse:

Rewrite the verse in your own words or personalize it.

Does this verse reveal anything about God/Jesus/Holy Spirit? Are there examples to follow or avoid?

How can I apply insights from this verse today? This week?

Notes, quotes, doodles, checklists, prayers, etc.

Genesis 34

Date:

Summarize the main idea(s) in this chapter:

Verse(s) that stood out:

Why did I pick this verse?

Definitions of words and/or cross references from my verse:

Rewrite the verse in your own words or personalize it.

Does this verse reveal anything about God/Jesus/Holy Spirit? Are there examples to follow or avoid?

How can I apply insights from this verse today? This week?

Notes, quotes, doodles, checklists, prayers, etc.

Genesis 35

Date:

Summarize the main idea(s) in this chapter:

Verse(s) that stood out:

Why did I pick this verse?

Definitions of words and/or cross references from my verse:

Rewrite the verse in your own words or personalize it.

Does this verse reveal anything about God/Jesus/Holy Spirit? Are there examples to follow or avoid?

How can I apply insights from this verse today? This week?

Notes, quotes, doodles, checklists, prayers, etc.

Review and reflect

Date:

Review each of the last six days work. Write or list the main takeaway you got from each chapter. (Look closely at the sections "What does this reveal about God?" and "How can I apply this?")

Are there any themes showing up in this week's work?

Are there any areas God is wanting to grow my faith or trust?
Are there any insights from this week's work on how to do this?

Are there any sins God is spotlighting in my life?
Are there any insights from this week's work on how to kill these sins?

Re-read one or two of the most impactful verses from this week and turn them into a prayer. (There is room on the next pages to write it down if you want.)

How can I thank or praise God as a result of what I've learned this week?

How can I apply what I've learned this week to my life today and next week?

Where do I need His strength for today? Tomorrow? Next week?

Is there a verse from this week that I should commit to memory? Write it on the next page or on a 3x5 card to take with you to memorize.

Are there any sins I need to confess to God in prayer?

Is there anyone I need to forgive? Is there anyone I need to ask forgiveness of?

Are there any seeds of bitterness starting to take root in my heart?

Are there any fears or worries I need to lay at His feet?

prayers, doodles, etc

Genesis 36

Date:

Summarize the main idea(s) in this chapter:

Verse(s) that stood out:

Why did I pick this verse?

Definitions of words and/or cross references from my verse:

Rewrite the verse in your own words or personalize it.

Does this verse reveal anything about God/Jesus/Holy Spirit? Are there examples to follow or avoid?

How can I apply insights from this verse today? This week?

Notes, quotes, doodles, checklists, prayers, etc.

Genesis 37

Date:

Summarize the main idea(s) in this chapter:

Verse(s) that stood out:

Why did I pick this verse?

Definitions of words and/or cross references from my verse:

Rewrite the verse in your own words or personalize it.

Does this verse reveal anything about God/Jesus/Holy Spirit? Are there examples to follow or avoid?

How can I apply insights from this verse today? This week?

Notes, quotes, doodles, checklists, prayers, etc.

Genesis 38

Date:

Summarize the main idea(s) in this chapter:

Verse(s) that stood out:

Why did I pick this verse?

Definitions of words and/or cross references from my verse:

Rewrite the verse in your own words or personalize it.

Does this verse reveal anything about God/Jesus/Holy Spirit? Are there examples to follow or avoid?

How can I apply insights from this verse today? This week?

Notes, quotes, doodles, checklists, prayers, etc.

Genesis 39-40

Date:

Summarize the main idea(s) in this chapter:

Verse(s) that stood out:

Why did I pick this verse?

Definitions of words and/or cross references from my verse:

Rewrite the verse in your own words or personalize it.

Does this verse reveal anything about God/Jesus/Holy Spirit? Are there examples to follow or avoid?

How can I apply insights from this verse today? This week?

Notes, quotes, doodles, checklists, prayers, etc.

Genesis 41

Date:

Summarize the main idea(s) in this chapter:

Verse(s) that stood out:

Why did I pick this verse?

Definitions of words and/or cross references from my verse:

Rewrite the verse in your own words or personalize it.

Does this verse reveal anything about God/Jesus/Holy Spirit? Are there examples to follow or avoid?

How can I apply insights from this verse today? This week?

Notes, quotes, doodles, checklists, prayers, etc.

Genesis 42

Date:

Summarize the main idea(s) in this chapter:

Verse(s) that stood out:

Why did I pick this verse?

Definitions of words and/or cross references from my verse:

Rewrite the verse in your own words or personalize it.

Does this verse reveal anything about God/Jesus/Holy Spirit? Are there examples to follow or avoid?

How can I apply insights from this verse today? This week?

Notes, quotes, doodles, checklists, prayers, etc.

Review and reflect

Date:

Review each of the last six days work. Write or list the main takeaway you got from each chapter. (Look closely at the sections "What does this reveal about God?" and "How can I apply this?")

Are there any themes showing up in this week's work?

Are there any areas God is wanting to grow my faith or trust?
Are there any insights from this week's work on how to do this?

Are there any sins God is spotlighting in my life?
Are there any insights from this week's work on how to kill these sins?

Re-read one or two of the most impactful verses from this week and turn them into a prayer. (There is room on the next pages to write it down if you want.)

How can I thank or praise God as a result of what I've learned this week?

How can I apply what I've learned this week to my life today and next week?

Where do I need His strength for today? Tomorrow? Next week?

Is there a verse from this week that I should commit to memory? Write it on the next page or on a 3x5 card to take with you to memorize.

Are there any sins I need to confess to God in prayer?

Is there anyone I need to forgive? Is there anyone I need to ask forgiveness of?

Are there any seeds of bitterness starting to take root in my heart?

Are there any fears or worries I need to lay at His feet?

prayers, doodles, etc

Genesis 43

Date:

Summarize the main idea(s) in this chapter:

Verse(s) that stood out:

Why did I pick this verse?

Definitions of words and/or cross references from my verse:

Rewrite the verse in your own words or personalize it.

Does this verse reveal anything about God/Jesus/Holy Spirit? Are there examples to follow or avoid?

How can I apply insights from this verse today? This week?

Notes, quotes, doodles, checklists, prayers, etc.

Genesis 44

Date:

Summarize the main idea(s) in this chapter:

Verse(s) that stood out:

Why did I pick this verse?

Definitions of words and/or cross references from my verse:

Rewrite the verse in your own words or personalize it.

Does this verse reveal anything about God/Jesus/Holy Spirit? Are there examples to follow or avoid?

How can I apply insights from this verse today? This week?

Notes, quotes, doodles, checklists, prayers, etc.

Genesis 45

Date:

Summarize the main idea(s) in this chapter:

Verse(s) that stood out:

Why did I pick this verse?

Definitions of words and/or cross references from my verse:

Rewrite the verse in your own words or personalize it.

Does this verse reveal anything about God/Jesus/Holy Spirit? Are there examples to follow or avoid?

How can I apply insights from this verse today? This week?

Notes, quotes, doodles, checklists, prayers, etc.

Genesis 46

Summarize the main idea(s) in this chapter:

Verse(s) that stood out:

Why did I pick this verse?

Definitions of words and/or cross references from my verse:

Rewrite the verse in your own words or personalize it.

Does this verse reveal anything about God/Jesus/Holy Spirit? Are there examples to follow or avoid?

How can I apply insights from this verse today? This week?

Notes, quotes, doodles, checklists, prayers, etc.

Genesis 47-48

Date:

Summarize the main idea(s) in this chapter:

Verse(s) that stood out:

Why did I pick this verse?

Definitions of words and/or cross references from my verse:

Rewrite the verse in your own words or personalize it.

Does this verse reveal anything about God/Jesus/Holy Spirit? Are there examples to follow or avoid?

How can I apply insights from this verse today? This week?

Notes, quotes, doodles, checklists, prayers, etc.

Genesis 49

Date:

Summarize the main idea(s) in this chapter:

Verse(s) that stood out:

Why did I pick this verse?

Definitions of words and/or cross references from my verse:

Rewrite the verse in your own words or personalize it.

Does this verse reveal anything about God/Jesus/Holy Spirit? Are there examples to follow or avoid?

How can I apply insights from this verse today? This week?

Notes, quotes, doodles, checklists, prayers, etc.

Review and reflect

Date:

Review each of the last six days work. Write or list the main takeaway you got from each chapter. (Look closely at the sections "What does this reveal about God?" and "How can I apply this?")

Are there any themes showing up in this week's work?

Are there any areas God is wanting to grow my faith or trust?
Are there any insights from this week's work on how to do this?

Are there any sins God is spotlighting in my life?
Are there any insights from this week's work on how to kill these sins?

Re-read one or two of the most impactful verses from this week and turn them into a prayer. (There is room on the next pages to write it down if you want.)

How can I thank or praise God as a result of what I've learned this week?

How can I apply what I've learned this week to my life today and next week?

Where do I need His strength for today? Tomorrow? Next week?

Is there a verse from this week that I should commit to memory? Write it on the next page or on a 3x5 card to take with you to memorize.

Are there any sins I need to confess to God in prayer?

Is there anyone I need to forgive? Is there anyone I need to ask forgiveness of?

Are there any seeds of bitterness starting to take root in my heart?

Are there any fears or worries I need to lay at His feet?

prayers, doodles, etc

Genesis 50

Date:

Summarize the main idea(s) in this chapter:

Verse(s) that stood out:

Why did I pick this verse?

Definitions of words and/or cross references from my verse:

Rewrite the verse in your own words or personalize it.

Does this verse reveal anything about God/Jesus/Holy Spirit? Are there examples to follow or avoid?

How can I apply insights from this verse today? This week?

Notes, quotes, doodles, checklists, prayers, etc.

 **Exodus 1-2**

Date:

Summarize the main idea(s) in this chapter:

Verse(s) that stood out:

Why did I pick this verse?

Definitions of words and/or cross references from my verse:

Rewrite the verse in your own words or personalize it.

Does this verse reveal anything about God/Jesus/Holy Spirit? Are there examples to follow or avoid?

How can I apply insights from this verse today? This week?

Notes, quotes, doodles, checklists, prayers, etc.

Exodus 3

Date:

Summarize the main idea(s) in this chapter:

Verse(s) that stood out:

Why did I pick this verse?

Definitions of words and/or cross references from my verse:

Rewrite the verse in your own words or personalize it.

Does this verse reveal anything about God/Jesus/Holy Spirit? Are there examples to follow or avoid?

How can I apply insights from this verse today? This week?

Notes, quotes, doodles, checklists, prayers, etc.

Exodus 4

Summarize the main idea(s) in this chapter:

Verse(s) that stood out:

Why did I pick this verse?

Definitions of words and/or cross references from my verse:

Rewrite the verse in your own words or personalize it.

Does this verse reveal anything about God/Jesus/Holy Spirit? Are there examples to follow or avoid?

How can I apply insights from this verse today? This week?

Notes, quotes, doodles, checklists, prayers, etc.

Exodus 5

Date:

Summarize the main idea(s) in this chapter:

Verse(s) that stood out:

Why did I pick this verse?

Definitions of words and/or cross references from my verse:

Rewrite the verse in your own words or personalize it.

Does this verse reveal anything about God/Jesus/Holy Spirit? Are there examples to follow or avoid?

How can I apply insights from this verse today? This week?

Notes, quotes, doodles, checklists, prayers, etc.

Exodus 6

Date:

Summarize the main idea(s) in this chapter:

Verse(s) that stood out:

Why did I pick this verse?

Definitions of words and/or cross references from my verse:

Rewrite the verse in your own words or personalize it.

Does this verse reveal anything about God/Jesus/Holy Spirit? Are there examples to follow or avoid?

How can I apply insights from this verse today? This week?

Notes, quotes, doodles, checklists, prayers, etc.

Review and reflect

Date:

Review each of the last six days work. Write or list the main takeaway you got from each chapter. (Look closely at the sections "What does this reveal about God?" and "How can I apply this?")

Are there any themes showing up in this week's work?

Are there any areas God is wanting to grow my faith or trust?
Are there any insights from this week's work on how to do this?

Are there any sins God is spotlighting in my life?
Are there any insights from this week's work on how to kill these sins?

Re-read one or two of the most impactful verses from this week and turn them into a prayer. (There is room on the next pages to write it down if you want.)

How can I thank or praise God as a result of what I've learned this week?

How can I apply what I've learned this week to my life today and next week?

Where do I need His strength for today? Tomorrow? Next week?

Is there a verse from this week that I should commit to memory? Write it on the next page or on a 3x5 card to take with you to memorize.

Are there any sins I need to confess to God in prayer?

Is there anyone I need to forgive? Is there anyone I need to ask forgiveness of?

Are there any seeds of bitterness starting to take root in my heart?

Are there any fears or worries I need to lay at His feet?

prayers, doodles, etc

Exodus 7

Summarize the main idea(s) in this chapter:

Verse(s) that stood out:

Why did I pick this verse?

Definitions of words and/or cross references from my verse:

Rewrite the verse in your own words or personalize it.

Does this verse reveal anything about God/Jesus/Holy Spirit? Are there examples to follow or avoid?

How can I apply insights from this verse today? This week?

Notes, quotes, doodles, checklists, prayers, etc.

Exodus 8

Date:

Summarize the main idea(s) in this chapter:

Verse(s) that stood out:

Why did I pick this verse?

Definitions of words and/or cross references from my verse:

Rewrite the verse in your own words or personalize it.

Does this verse reveal anything about God/Jesus/Holy Spirit? Are there examples to follow or avoid?

How can I apply insights from this verse today? This week?

Notes, quotes, doodles, checklists, prayers, etc.

Exodus 9

Date:

Summarize the main idea(s) in this chapter:

Verse(s) that stood out:

Why did I pick this verse?

Definitions of words and/or cross references from my verse:

Rewrite the verse in your own words or personalize it.

Does this verse reveal anything about God/Jesus/Holy Spirit? Are there examples to follow or avoid?

How can I apply insights from this verse today? This week?

Notes, quotes, doodles, checklists, prayers, etc.

Exodus 10

Date:

Summarize the main idea(s) in this chapter:

Verse(s) that stood out:

Why did I pick this verse?

Definitions of words and/or cross references from my verse:

Rewrite the verse in your own words or personalize it.

Does this verse reveal anything about God/Jesus/Holy Spirit? Are there examples to follow or avoid?

How can I apply insights from this verse today? This week?

Notes, quotes, doodles, checklists, prayers, etc.

Exodus 11

Summarize the main idea(s) in this chapter:

Verse(s) that stood out:

Why did I pick this verse?

Definitions of words and/or cross references from my verse:

Rewrite the verse in your own words or personalize it.

Does this verse reveal anything about God/Jesus/Holy Spirit? Are there examples to follow or avoid?

How can I apply insights from this verse today? This week?

Notes, quotes, doodles, checklists, prayers, etc.

Exodus 12

Summarize the main idea(s) in this chapter:

Verse(s) that stood out:

Why did I pick this verse?

Definitions of words and/or cross references from my verse:

Rewrite the verse in your own words or personalize it.

Does this verse reveal anything about God/Jesus/Holy Spirit? Are there examples to follow or avoid?

How can I apply insights from this verse today? This week?

Notes, quotes, doodles, checklists, prayers, etc.

Review and reflect

Date:

Review each of the last six days work. Write or list the main takeaway you got from each chapter. (Look closely at the sections "What does this reveal about God?" and "How can I apply this?")

Are there any themes showing up in this week's work?

Are there any areas God is wanting to grow my faith or trust?
Are there any insights from this week's work on how to do this?

Are there any sins God is spotlighting in my life?
Are there any insights from this week's work on how to kill these sins?

Re-read one or two of the most impactful verses from this week and turn them into a prayer. (There is room on the next pages to write it down if you want.)

How can I thank or praise God as a result of what I've learned this week?

How can I apply what I've learned this week to my life today and next week?

Where do I need His strength for today? Tomorrow? Next week?

Is there a verse from this week that I should commit to memory? Write it on the next page or on a 3x5 card to take with you to memorize.

Are there any sins I need to confess to God in prayer?

Is there anyone I need to forgive? Is there anyone I need to ask forgiveness of?

Are there any seeds of bitterness starting to take root in my heart?

Are there any fears or worries I need to lay at His feet?

prayers, doodles, etc

Congratulations!

You did it! Great job on finishing. Look for Volume Two on Amazon to continue your journey through the Bible!

Also be sure to check out the Journal and Doodle Bible studies on Amazon and on my website www.StoneSoupforFive.com. These inductive Bible studies work through a book of the Bible with built in meditation, questions, doodles, and much more.

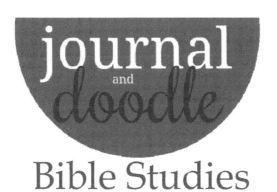

Bible Studies

www.StoneSoupforFive.com

77919507R00120

Made in the USA
San Bernardino, CA
30 May 2018